HOW TO SELL YOUR HOUSE
WITHOUT A REAL ESTATE AGENT!

BY ZACHARY ROUSE

©2014 by **Zachary Rouse**
Published by **CreditorWeekly, LLC**
Unauthorized Reproduction Prohibited
http://zacharyrouse.com

HOW TO SELL YOUR HOUSE
WITHOUT A REAL ESTATE AGENT!
By Zachary Rouse
Oregon Real Estate Broker

©2014 by Zachary Rouse
Published by CreditorWeekly, LLC
Unauthorized Reproduction Prohibited
http://zacharyrouse.com

INTRODUCTION

Hi, Homeowner! My name is Zachary Rouse. I'm a real estate broker in Portland, Oregon. Residential and mutli-family property sales are my specialty. I love seeing people succeed at their financial goals, and that's why I started working with home buyers and sellers. Recently, I discovered that there is a shortage of high-quality information for home sellers who want to cut out that pesky middle-man, and get their full price for their property.

Seeing a growing number of residential properties for-sale-by-owner on hundreds of online sites around the country and the world, I thought it might be helpful to give the entrepreneurial homeowner a step-by-step guide for how to DIY your house sale. So I have written this easy-to-follow book that will take you through the daunting and exciting world of selling your house.

"What's the catch?", I hear you say. There is no catch. Just information. Enjoy this book, and don't hesitate to shoot me an email at zack@summapdx.com to let me know you liked it. I'm always available to talk about the exciting world of real estate! And check out my website for up-to-date listings in the Portland, OR area, and my informative blog. It's all available at zacharyrouse.com.

Selling a house is time-consuming, complicated, and sometimes legally dangerous. But if you have the time, the gumption, and the interest in learning a whole lot really quickly, you could save yourself thousands of dollars! If you are up to the task, then let's get to brass tacks! You'll be on a beach in no time.

"Without a little elbow grease, knowitall, and ignorance, we would still be a bunch of poor saps staring at the wall of the cave" - Anonymous

CHAPTER 1. Research

Your first order of business in getting ready to sell your house FSBO(for-sale-by-owner) is to do some research on what actually transpires in a real estate transaction. Now, unless your grandpapa willed you his home, you bought your house, so you will be familiar with the buyer's side of the deal. But when it comes to selling, it's a whole other ball of wax. There are disclosures, encumbrances and leins to deal with, permits for past work on the house that never got pulled, title history investigations, tax declarations, mortgage wraparound negotiations, repair addenda, tenants and occupants, city ordinances allowing and restricting certain kinds of land usages, contingent offers; the list goes on and on. And that's just the tip of the iceberg.

There are many variables in a real estate transaction. My favorite quote, which is completely un-related to real estate, but so applicable, is from former Secretary of Defense Donald Rumsfeld:

"There are known knowns. These are things we know that we know. There are known unknowns. That is to say, there are things that we know we don't know. But there are also unknown unknowns. There are things we don't know we don't know."

Truer words were never spoken about a real estate transaction. Something will inevitably come up on a Tuesday morning when you're at work, and because the issue is time-sensitive, you'll have to leave work to go down to the city assessor's office to pick up a piece of paperwork (you know how the gears of bureaucracy work!), and BOOM! There goes your day. Us real estate agents deal with these variables so you don't have to. But we get the big bucks for it, too. Sometimes, we get as much as 3% of your total sale price. Depending on the house, that can be upwards of five or six thousand dollars or more. If you are willing to take it on, then you don't need an agent working for you.

Since you've been through the experience at least once, pull out the paperwork and contracts on your home and read them thoroughly. Learn the language of real estate, and read a few books about how to sell your house. Like this one! Do some research on the terminology of contracts. For example, what's the difference between a Land Sales Contract and a Lease Option? What's a Cash Sale v. a Conventionally funded transaction? What's an FHA loan, and who qualifies for it? How about a VA loan? Can a veteran buy your house? Are you a veteran? Can you sell your house to a non-veteran? Can a non-veteran assume a veteran's home loan?

TIDBIT: If your home is worth more than $417,000, your buyer will need to obtain what is called a "Jumbo" loan. *CHALLENGE*: You might get a great offer on your place. More than asking! You'll say, "OMG! I'm gonna be rich!" You get half-way through Escrow, and you learn that you accepted an offer from someone who couldn't afford the loan they were promising they could get! Time to go back to the drawing board.

Gather all the paperwork and forms you'll need to complete your real estate transaction. This includes

1. **Sales Agreement Forms.** There are many forms involved in the sale of your home. Do an internet search for providers of these forms. It is important that you use state-approved forms, as they have all of the required legal language necessary for a fully legal sale of your property. There is a number of websites which provide a subscription plan that will grant you access to all the forms you will need. Some require licensing to use, and others do not.

2. **Copies of all property records** for the numerous appraisers and

inspectors who will be coming over to your house to make sure everything is in order.

3. **Title History.** You obtain a Title History, or a Trio, from your Title and Escrow company, for a fee. They provide you with a comprehensive report on the history of your home's deeds, titles, leins and encumbrances, rites of passage, mineral and airspace rights, and more. They help you discover any potential legal and bureaucratic pitfalls before you close your house and walk away. This protects you from future problems that might be associated with your name once you've sold the house.

4. **Insurance documents.** Home owner's insurance, title insurance, etc... Gather all of your statements for the entire time you have owned the property. This paperwork is important for the buyer to see that there has been a clear ownership record, and keeps you safe from errors and omissions.

5. **Disclosures and legal documents.** There is a number of disclosure documents that must be filled out correctly in order for you to sell your house. These include, but are not limited to:

    Property Disclosure – This is a long-form that is a checklist of nearly every aspect of your property, from the condition of the foundation to the pipes, to the roof's condition, and much more. It is critical that this is filled out correctly to protect you, the SELLER, from liability.

    Lead Based Paint Disclosure - give buyers a pamphlet prepared by the U.S. Environmental Protection Agency (EPA) called *Protect Your Family from Lead in Your Home*

    Repairs

    Termites

    Water Damage/Mold

    Natural and Environmental Hazards – This includes soil examinations, lead pipe mitigations, water quality surveys, electro-magnetic field studies, and more.

    Infamous Past – Not to be morbid. But did someone die in your house? Murder? Ghosts? Arson? Make sure you know the history or your property backward and forward, and disclose every possible infamous event. Protect your name and yourself from potential lawsuits down the line.

Septic/Cistern

Underground Tanks – Oil heaters in older homes will often have underground oil tanks that need an EPA-sanctioned clean-up effort reminiscent of a Superfund site - in order to clear your title for sale.

· Radon – Radon is a colorless, odorless gas that sits very close to the ground underneath many parts of the country's houses. You must disclose if you have high levels of Radon underneath your home.

There are more disclosures that will be necessary than I have room in this book to list. Do your "due diligence", and research all of the necessary disclosures that the law of your state requires. I am a real estate agent, but I'm not omniscient. If you are going to sell your house without me, then you will need to do my job yourself. It is doable, but takes time and effort to do it correctly. You'll also want to check and recheck every form you fill out for errors or omissions. Establish a habit early on of being anal about the process. It will save you the heartache that so many FSBO sellers that came before you have suffered.

> **TIDBIT**: Houses built before 1974 will have asbestos insulation. If this asbestos gets loose and flaky, it becomes a disaster. It is critical that you know the status of your home's asbestos situation. If it hasn't already been removed, you are looking at a $20-30,000 removal operation just in order to sell your house. This disclosure is a very important one.

6. **Hire a real estate attorney.** Unfortunately, in this sue-happy modern world we live in, a home buyer can sue you for many things. The main things you can be sued for by the purchaser of your home are errors or omissions. This means that at some point, whether intentionally or unintentionally, you misrepresented the state of your property, by either not disclosing, or wrongly describing a "material fact" relating to your property and its marketability (ability to be brought to market). Sometimes home sellers get sued for more money than they even made on the sale in the

first place! What a bummer. This is why it is very important to have the knowledge of your favorite real estate attorney at the ready. Real estate agents carry what is known as E and O insurance, or Errors and Omissions insurance. This protects us against any potential errors that may occur during the sale of real property. Since you aren't using an agent, in trade for that broker's fee is your increased obligation to do "due diligence", or to do your research. If you don't have this insurance, you'd better cross those t's and dot those i's!

7. **Hire an appraiser**. Appraisers help you market your property. The way they do this is that they inspect your property, survey its particular benefits and detractions; they do research on the neighborhood, many comparable properties to yours, and what they sold for in the recent past; compare amenities and histories, and more. They come up with an assessment of your property's marketable valuation. This allows a bank or other lending institution to feel comfortable lending the money you are asking the buyer to pay for your house. Appraisers generally tend to come in lower than what you think your property is worth.

Part of that is the psychology of market dynamics. The seller always tends to believe that their product is worth more than the market will bear. And buyers will generally see the product as worth less than the market indicates. This is why when you sell your house by yourself, you need to think like ME! That's right. You have to ignore the fact that your house was home to your children and comforted your family during holidays and celebrations, hardships and recoveries from injury. You have to act like it's just a deal. If you can do that, then you will find the right balance to get it sold without ME! You can do it.

The other reason they tend to come in lower than you think they should is that there is a tension between previous market conditions and future, anticipated market conditions. The appraiser is looking at many more factors than you or I can fathom. As a result, they will get a different number than you will.
8.

9. **Consider how you want to structure the deal.** Will you want to offer your buyers any incentives such as owner-financing (owner carry), or lease-to-own, or lease option, to make the deal more attractive to a buyer? Learn how these arrangements work. Purchase a book on the different types of real estate transactions, and see which one best fits your needs and desires. If you are just DONE with your house, then the best option is probably a cash/conventional sale. If you don't mind hanging around for

five or ten years while collecting a nice monthly paycheck, an owner carry might do you just fine. Each type of transaction has its own unique properties, and legal and logistical challenges. Find the one that seems easiest. I find, the path of least resistence is usually the right path.

HOME IMPROVEMENTS THAT PAY YOU BACK

1. Remodeling the Kitchen
60%–120%

You can expect to recoup 60%–120% of your investment on a kitchen remodel, as long as you don't go overboard. You should never make your kitchen fancier than the rest of the house, or the neighborhood.

2. Bathroom Addition
80%–130%

If your home only has one bathroom, you can recoup a large chunk of your investment by adding another one. It is estimated that you can recoup 80%–130% of whatever you spend adding a bathroom.

3. Adding Square Footage
50%–83%

Adding more square footage to your home with a new room can be an incredibly expensive project. However, you can typically recoup between 50% and 83% of your initial investment. Just make sure you keep costs under control.

4. Deck Addition
65%–90%

If you make your deck and your backyard more appealing, your house will be more appealing to prospective buyers when you decide to sell. Homeowners can recoup 65%–90% of their investment by adding a deck.

CALIFORNIA ASSOCIATION OF REALTORS®

Source: Moneycrashers.com

CHAPTER 2. Preparation

Now turn your entrepreneurial spirit toward your home. Your marketing problems will fall into three categories:

Cosmetic problems;
Functional issues; and
Things you can't (or won't) fix.

The first two must be dealt with before you go out and try to sell your property, and the third, if any, will be addressed when you decide what price to ask for your home.

Look truly critically at your house. Many things that you were willing to live with, or that weren't an issue because you were renting the place out, now become make-or-break items to a buyer. These are the Cosmetic issues that will make all the difference between you getting market value for your property, or instead getting ridiculously low offers (a la craigslist), or even no offers at all. Paint over scuffs on the walls. Clean the baseboards and doorjambs. Hire a professional window washer to come in and do a pro job on your glass surfaces. Choose colors to paint over brightly colored walls in neutrals. Neutral colors are more attractive to a buyer because they appear more general, which allows for the buyer to use her/his imagination in seeing him/herself living in the house. Resurface the hardwood floors with a sander. If you don't want to hire a finish carpenter to come in, go to Home Depot and rent a sander, and spend a few days sanding down those beautiful floors and do a refinish. A newly done hardwood floor can up your home's value by tens of thousands of dollars. It can take upwards of two weeks of hard work, but will increase your valuation markedly. Dump that old carpet in lew of hardwood or laminate flooring. There is some laminate flooring now that costs one dollar per square foot. If you have the warewithall to put them in yourself, you can make a simple and cheap improvement look like a thirty thousand dollar renovation. Take the time to perfect the cosmetic appearance of your home. You are truly not ready to sell your home by yourself until you have a product that your customer wants.

Now look at the functional things in your house. What needs to be repaired? What have you been putting up with that now just needs to GO? There's always something that you didn't really mind dealing with: the handle on the fridge falling off every time you open the door; the doorknob on the back door only turning right but not left; the shower head squirting out the side against the wall. These things, believe it or not, can be make-or-break to an aesthetically minded buyer! Go over your appliances with a fine tooth comb. Make sure that your refrigerator is operating at its most efficient. Clean the dust off of the air intake on the back, which is a common cause of fridges dying; Inspect the heater. Is your heater high-efficiency? If not, it's time for a replacement. Everyone has a high-efficiency furnace now. It's standard in homes. And yours is no exception. The first item in the repair addendum from your buyer after inspections will be an upgrade on the furnace. No one likes the cold winter, and no one likes a $400 heating bill. Check the air conditioning. If it's fall or spring, turn it on and make sure it's running correctly. Call your repair company and order a routine maintenance on the unit. Make sure all your appliances work perfectly when you close the door for the last time and say goodbye. It's what your buyer will expect from you, and it's what you'll expect from your next seller.

The Roof: The roof is a big one. If it's five years old or newer, great! Make sure you clean your gutters out to avoid build-up and poor drainage. If your roof is older than five years, then it needs to be well-inspected for leaks, tears, and other irregularities that could lead to damage to the frame or truss of your home.

Finally, really examine the things that you can't, or won't, change about your house. Is a new roof necessary, but just not on your list of doable repairs? Is there black mold in your walls, but you're not in a financial position to be tearing walls out to get to it? Is it on a busy corner or street, next to a farm, or an auto mechanic's shop? Or is it on a weirdly shaped lot, facing your neighbor's kitchen window? Is its layout strange because of decades of ad-ons and renovations that changed the original floorplan? You may need to lower the price to make your property interesting to real buyers. Since you are doing the sale yourself, it will be critical for you to be aware of ALL of these items, so that you can counter any potential criticisms from a buyer hoping to score a better deal from you. The negotiation process is intense, and you will need to be steely, and a master of your emotions before entering into the negotiating phase with a buyer or, more often than not, a seasoned buyer's agent.

Next Step: Get to the cleaning! Have you been storing old Vogue or Sports Illustraded magazines? Do you have every issue from 1987? Got to go!

Are you a novice woodworker with ten unfinished projects in the garage? Got to go! Do you have a 4,640cc V8 block from your favorite '57 Chevy in the back yard? Got to go! Do you love to collect art? Got to go. Do you have any cars that don't run? Got to go. Clean out every corner of your property. If you've been an avid composter for fifteen years and have a wonderful pile of steaming garden love in the corner of your yard...Got to go. Get it?

It's not personal. And that is the point. It's business. Pure and simple. It's emotional, it's challenging, it's sometimes trying! But it will be worth it in the end when you walk away from your old home clean of the material, and emotional, clutter that has been plaguing you for your tenureship in your house. Your house is now a product that you are bringing to market. Do you get emotional when you trade stocks? No! There's a reason for that: You are distanced from the mayhem. You get to sit back and look at the numbers scroll across the screen, and call your stock trader up on the phone and say, "It's down twenty points! What are you doing??? Sell that bad boy!" When you sell your house yourself, you take that distance away, and you are now getting up close and personal with your own situation. It's beautiful and hard. Get to it!

TIDBIT: Did you know that real estate agents "STAGE" houses? That's right! We hire companies that specialize in furnishing homes temporarily, so that they will look enticing to potential buyers. This can cost upwards of a thousand dollars. They bring in couches, bistro tables and stools, wet bars, art, drapes, lamps and fixtures. Sometimes, a staging will include replacement of fixtures in the house temporarily, just to improve the showing capability of the home!

Re-arrange your house so that air flow is at its best. Put furniture in a configuration that will allow for the most amount of light, and the easiest passage for buyers through the rooms. Aim for crisp, uncluttered interiors, rooms and closets. Trim your apple tree, wash your garage windows, remove any of your big heavy drapes. It won't cost you any money, and it opens up your space, whether it's a small WWII breadbox, or a cavernous post-modern ranch. Cleaning out everything that is not necessary to showing the house will make your home/product seem bright and spacious. You're ready to sell your house. Make it ready to be occupied and re-designed by its new owner.

CHAPTER 3. Price Your House

The biggest mistake home sellers make is pricing their product too high. You raised your family in it. It's priceless to you! But it's really not any more or any less valuable to the market than what it will fetch from a buyer. If you put the price too high, you could stop people from looking at it before they even know what a gem you know it is. If it is priced too high, you may not know it until it's too late.

You could have it for sale for two months, and no one is calling you. Because they look at the pictures of your house, and of other comparable houses on the market, and they pass yours right up. Many people are selling the exact same thing that you have. The difference is in the price. Price is King.

A buyer might love the look and feel of your clean, sparkly house, but say to their agent, "It's just priced thirty thousand above market value". And the agent will say, "Just wait. It'll come down once they realize that they've over-priced it." And guess what? They're right.

> **TIDBIT:** Often, an over-priced launch causes the property to sell at below market value. Seems crazy, right? It's true.

You're sitting there, your house is on the market for two, three months, and you drop the price one, two, three times, until finally you've dropped it $30,000! And NOW, and only now, do you start to see inquiries trickle in. Make no mistake: Those people saw your house two months ago. They just didn't bite, because it was priced too high. They waited you out. And now, they have the upper hand. They'll come in with an offer even lower than the lowest price you ever thought you'd go for, and, having waited months to get any interest in it, and feeling desperate, you will take the first low-ball offer that comes in. You lose. Bad move.

To determine what you consider the home's fair market value, research neighborhood sales from the past one year. Attend open houses and check out the competition. Speak with the agents at these open houses about what the neighborhood market is doing, what that particular house is going for, do they really think it's priced right, or high, or low. Get their expertise. Use as many data points as you can to get a starting idea. You can interview real estate agents, but be honest about your intention to try to sell the house yourself. Some may not want to spend the time to speak with you, but many agents like me will know that you still might need an agent sometime in the future, and we will welcome the chance to talk shop with you. Don't forget to sign up for blog feeds regarding your local real estate scene. There are many agents blogging every day about new regulations, market changes, flood plain re-assignments, and more. You can learn much from these blogs, and there are plenty of knowledgeable agents out there who will inadvertantly teach you how to do their job for free.

If you are stumped, hire an appraiser. A professional appraisal could cost you between $300 to $700. And having that report in your hands is like gold when you're negotiating with a low-baller, or a buyer's lending institution that is trying not to lend market value on your property. Remember what I said earlier about appraisers tending to come in low. This is the risk you take when you go it alone. But the rewards, if you have the time and energy to do the research, could be in the thousands of dollars, not to mention a vastly increased knowledge base regarding real estate sales. Who knows? You may even decide to become licensed in real estate yourself, because you will have already done all the work to figure it all out! Finally, if you are still unsure about how to come up with your listing price, email me, and I will send you a CMA (a comparative market analysis), for free. ziggidyone@gmail.com is my personal email, and you are welcome to send me a message with your name, address, and the request for a CMA, and I'll send you a market analysis in PDF format. Make sure to let me know how you enjoyed reading this book in your message. I love feedback, because it allows me to constantly improve my performance in this dynamic, exciting industry.

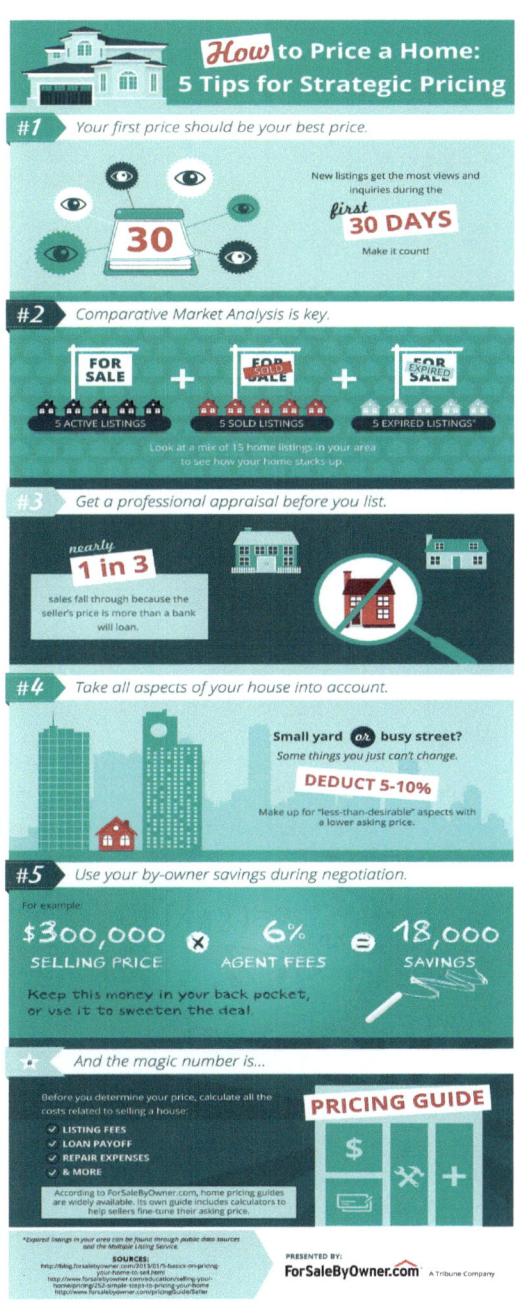

CHAPTER 4. Market Your House

The internet, in all its glorious splendor of magical zero's and one's, has all but removed from the equation what, in the past, was a real estate agent's golden ticket: the MLS (multiple listing service). For a fee about a third of what it costs to hire an agent, you can now list your FSBO house on an MLS, and get similar exposure to the market, without having to pay the full brokers' commission when your sale closes. You don't get service, but you do get to show your house to thousands of potential buyers and buyers' agents.

Something to watch out for when listing FSBO on an MLS is that you will be contacted by many agents who may or may not have buyers for your property. They will all profess to have found your buyer. They may have, or they may not have. Either way, you'll either be fending off subtle and not-so subtle attempts at listing your property, or you'll be negotiating directly with a broker, who went to school for real estate, knows the market inside and out, including all the tricks that come with this knowledge, and you'll need to be very careful about dealing with an agent without representation. There are many pitfalls and traps that you will need to learn about before getting into a negotiation with an agent, whose job it is to get their client the very best deal possible, even to your detriment.

One way to entice agents with buyers, and cut out their interest in trying to list your property, is to offer a "Courtesy to Agents". This is a fee that you pay the buyer's agent for bringing you the buyer for your place. It's usually half of the total brokers' commissions in the current market. For instance, if you offer a "Broker Courtesy" of 3%, you will have brokers looking for buyers for your property. We may not be coming out of the woodwork, because of the work we know we'll have to do in order to make the deal happen. We know that because you are a home owner, and not an agent, the onus will most likely fall on us to do the paperwork for both sides in order to make sure the transaction transpires properly and legally. But the chance is always there. Brokers want to do deals. Offer us a doable deal, and we will work on it.

TIDBIT: Real estate agents are known as "Fiduciaries". This means that we put our clients' needs above our own. Our legal and moral responsibility is to fight for our clients' interests before our own. This makes us great negotiators.

Other platforms, including craigslist, zillow, trulia, websites geared exclusively to FSBO's, attract people looking for their new house. If you use these platforms to market and sell your home, make sure the sites you use pull a large number of unique visitors to their sites each day. You don't want to pay for a subscription to a platform that doesn't see a lot of eyes coming to it. A lot of sites claim to have impressive traffic but actually are just shell sites that don't have much functionality to them, but steal your information and market to your inbox on an hourly basis.

Also, you need to become up-to-speed on the social networking sites, which are a wonderful way to connect you to potential customers for your product without seeming like you are selling something. There's a new social media site every five minutes. Facebook is just the tip of the iceberg. There are new ones constantly popping up, and they have such good indexing in the search engines that they quickly have hundreds of millions of visitors per day! This is a potential goldmine for your efforts to get your house sold. Comment on people's statuses regularly and often.

Post many pictures of your newly beautified place on these social media websites. Don't say why you've beautified. Just wait and let your friends comment on how gorgeous your new place is. When they ask you, "Are you selling your house or something?", say "Yes. As a matter of fact, I am. Why? Are you interested?"

Mike will post twenty-three pictures of his new Chocolate Lab, Stewart. Pictures of Stewart running on the beach (where you'd rather be). Pictures of Stewart leaping to catch a stick the size of the Douglas Fir in your front yard. Pictures of a huge-tongued Stewart cuddling by the fire with Mike, and Mike's less-than elated fiancee. And you may have recently read that this happy young couple is looking for a yard big enough for this beast named Stewart to romp and dig in. Don't miss the opportunity to let Mike know that you love Chocolate Labs, and not only that, you just happen to be thinking of putting your place on the market. And what's more, when *your* kids were growing up, they had a

Golden Retreiver who loved chasing squirrels around the spacious yard you've got. See what I mean? You could have just found your buyer by spending a little time looking at puppy pix on the internet. All of a sudden, what seemed like a waste of time, got you one step closer to that beach we were talking about. There's a margarita in your future, I can feel it.

One market for the Broker Courtesy is the first-time home buyer, who uses an agent. They may need special terms to make it happen, and the broker is excited to make the deal happen for the buyer. She/He will win that house for his/her client, and you get your house sold as a result.

Call all of your friends. Someone is looking for what you have. Your sister in-law's co-worker at the plant has a growing family and needs a basement. It's also a chance for you to catch up with what your friends and family have been doing since you last spoke. Ask them how they're doing. Find out what their kids have been up to. THEN start talking about what you're up to: You're selling your house. That's big news. Tell them the details. It's a three bedroom, one bath ranch in a quiet neighborhood two miles from the easily accessible freeway! How far from downtown is your place? You know the traffic conditions, you know where the parks are, you know where Baskin Robbins is, you know where the closest safe bar is. You know where the Chinese restaurant is, and it's within walking distance. Communicate its special features, and be proud of the work you've done to make it a great place to live. Be honest about why you're moving. No one needs to be lied to. They need the truth of what they're getting themselves into. It's not a used car. It's a lifestyle. And yours has been lovely and will be the same for your buyer.

Buy an ad in the local newspaper's online issue. It will cost $150 to $300, but you will have a circulation of thousands of people who come to the site every day for a week-long period, and they will be seeing your house for sale by owner. You will most certainly get calls, if not offers, from this effort.

Do you have a website? If so, revamp it to feature the fact that you are selling your house. Post pictures that link to your ad on zillow, craigslist, or whatever platforms you are using. And likewise, post links to your website on all the social media sites that you belong to. The more opportunities you have for people to cross link and arrive at something talking about your house, which just happens to be for sale, the more chance you will have of finding your buyer.

Buy a google ad. This is a complicated, frustrating endeavor. Because the internal workings of the adwords part of google are like an alien world that no one of our kind has ever visited before, you will feel like you are taking crazy pills the whole way through. You will click on links that lead you nowhere, sign up for things you never knew existed or that you would ever need; and you'll try to kill your computer half-way through the process of getting your account set up. But it really is worth it in the end. You can bid a price on your keywords, and set your own advertising budget so that it doesn't go over a certain dollar amount per day, and you can make your ad link to your website. So when someone goes to google and searches for "3 bedroom, 1 bath craftsman in Laurelhurst" (a beautiful neighborhood in Portland, OR), your ad will appear out of the ethers magically, and they will click on it. This will send them directly to your website, where you have all the beautiful pictures and blurbs about your *product*. They will fall in love with your house, call you, and offer twenty thousand above asking, immediately! Well, maybe it's not that easy. But it's another avenue for marketing that you really need if you're going to do this by yourself.

If you have a question, or idea that you think might work to market your property but are unsure of its viability, shoot me an email and run it by me! I always have time to hear from my readers, and would love to find out what new, innovative entrepreneurs like yourself are doing to get your houses sold.

BUYING & SELLING WALKABILITY

We all know that walking is good for us, but it can also be very important when buying or selling a home. Walk scores are determined based on the proximity of amenities such as restaurants and shops, and community hubs such as schools, parks, and libraries. Walk scores range from 0 to 100, and any rating above 70 is considered "very walkable." To check a walk score in a specific city or neighborhood, visit: **www.walkscore.com**.

BUYING in a walkable neighborhood has several benefits.

LOSE WEIGHT!
The average resident of a walkable neighborhood weighs 6 to 10 pounds less than someone who lives in a car-dependent neighborhood.

SAVE MONEY!
Transportation is the second largest expense for American households, costing more than food, clothing, and health care.

CONNECT!
Studies show that for every 10 minutes a person spends in a daily car commute, time spent in community activities falls by 10%.

SELLING in a walkable neighborhood is also advantageous. A recent study by CEOs for Cities found that higher walk scores are directly linked to higher home values.

$4,000 - $34,000 more

ONE WALK POINT EQUALS
$700 TO $3,000
more in home value, depending on the market.

Homes with above-average walk scores are worth between $4,000 to $34,000 more than similar but less walkable homes.

CALIFORNIA'S 3 MOST WALKABLE CITIES:
- ALBANY
- SAN FRANCISCO
- WEST HOLLYWOOD

Sources: Walkscore.com; *Walking the Walk*, a study by CEOs for Cities; the National Complete Streets Coalition; and a study linking walkability and fitness by the University of Utah

7 Tips To Sell PROPERTIES ONLINE

#1 Create Listing on Blog Page:
Once you have a property under contract, you'll want to enter all the information, upload photos and videos to this site. All other forms of media placed on different sites should link back to your blog page.

#2 Create Videos:
Creating a video walkthrough will allow potential buyers to experience your home better than any words or pictures could ever describe

#3 Promote on multiple online sites:
Take advantage of these sites and fill out all information completely. Remember to link back to your site

#4 Post on Craigslist:
Craigslist is a great place to post to get you found online.

#5 Promote Socially:
Anytime you create a video, you should upload to your YouTube Page. Other social sites good for real estate include Pinterest, Facebook, Google+ and Twitter.

#6 Create Press Release:
Press releases are a phenomenal way to move up the search engines. The best part is that you can write and promote for free.

#7 Online REI Clubs:
Many real estate investing clubs will allow you to post properties that you have for sale. This type of promotion can be very valuable if your end buyer is an investor.

Source:
http://www.reimaverick.com/how-to-sell-real-estate-online/

Brought to you by
REImaverick.com

CHAPTER5. Negotiating

The time will come. You will get an offer on your house. But beware! The devil is in the details. It might have contingencies and addenda.

Number One is Buyer preapproval. If your buyer is not pre-approved for the loan that they are promising they will get, you do not have a deal. Until the money is there, and the money is hard to get, you do not have a deal. Make sure that your buyer attaches their lender preapproval letter to any offer that you are considering. Do not accept any offer without a preapproval letter. You could get two days from closing, and find out that your buyer lost their job, and can't actually get a loan. Back to the drawing board.

Of course, this can happen anyway, if anything at all changes between the time that your buyer gets their preapproval letter and closing. If their grandmama puts sixty thousand dollars in their account and moves to Alaska to say hello to nature, your buyer's preapproval will be invalidated. That's right! Even MORE money in your buyer's account can joepardize your house sale.

Number Two is the Earnest Money Agreement, also known as the Sale Agreement. You must get an earnest money deposit prior to accepting any offer.

TIDBIT: Earnest Money is a deposit that a buyer puts into an escrow account to make you, the seller, feel more secure that you actually have a buyer and not some fly-by-night who can't even get a loan. The earnest money can take the form of a check, cashier's check, money order, or even a promissory note, which is just a piece of signed paper promising to pay the earnest money upon your acceptance of the offer.

Your buyer might make an offer on your house, but want to close in ninety days, instead of the usual thirty to forty-five day escrow period. What's up? Why ninety? Are you pulling a fast one?

Dave and Susie Jones can't buy your house until they have closed on the sale of their condo in Bethesda. They want you to wait until they find *their* buyer. If you accept their offer, you're stuck. You can't sell to someone else. You just have to wait. All the while keeping your place clean and ready for sale. They might not want to put any earnest money down until they get theirs sold first. Maybe all their cash is tied up in their condo.

There may be slightly hidden clauses in the offer. They may want you to resurface all the floors and replace the vanity in the guest bathroom. This could cost thousands, even eat up your whole return. Make sure you read through the entire offer that someone gives you. They are going to give you the kitchen sink in terms of requests. It's your responsibility to know what is doable and what is not. If you don't want to do the vanity, you don't have to.

An offer is just that. An offer. But it's also a contract. If you accept an offer from a buyer, by signing the offer you have obligated the buyer and yourself to the written contract that you have received.

Each tier of offer and counteroffer is a separate and attached contract. If you like everything about the buyer's offer except the bathroom vanity, you must reject their first offer and submit to them a counteroffer that is identical to theirs, simply omitting the vanity replacement. They, then, have the right to reject your counteroffer, and you no longer have a deal. Often, there are many counteroffers that transpire during the process of a real estate transaction. They often boil down to minute details that you thought could be verbally resolved, but that require signatures from three or more people, scans and emails of multiple copies of documents, acceptance of terms by initial and signatures, bureaucrat's signatures on work that has been completed, and more. Often, the escrow period, which just means the period of time that the transaction can still be cancelled, the time between acceptance of an offer and closing, must be extended to allow for unexpected contingencies that arise on either end of the transaction.

Recently, I was the listing agent on a duplex, which is both a residence and a multi-family property. The buyer put in their offer, and my client accepted it. During the escrow period, the buyer's agent detected a strange smell coming from below the back unit of the duplex. Luckily the unit was unoccupied. The neighbor in the front unit also noticed the scent, and had been feeling nauseous for a number of days. The sale was at risk because of this smell. I had to convince the not-so-wealthy owner to arrange for a plumber to come assess and fix the source of this smell. Turned out, there was a hole in the sewer line between the kitchen sink and the main sewer line leading to the street. They had to replace the entire joint between the property's sewer line and the city's. Then they had to clean up the raw sewage that had accumulated on the plastic vapor barrier on the ground below the house. Then they had to replace the plastic vapor barrier itself. Three thousand dollars and another week were added to the seller's responsibility. These negotiations are something that real estate agents are paid to deal with.

If you don't know everything, and you won't: then you must prepare yourself for contingencies such as these. Because they WILL happen. There is nothing you can do about it. You just have to suck it up and move on. Once you are in contract, you are obligated to do what is necessary to create clear and marketable title for your property's sale. If you miss one detail, you can be sued for errors and omissions, and end up spending your margarita money on a lawyer's margarita.

Be prepared for numerous offers and counteroffers on your home sale. You will get offers that expire in three hours. If you are slow to react to the offer, or don't check your email for a few hours because you're in an office meeting or seminar, or because you are on your roof replacing tiles so you can sell your house, you will lose your sale. Because your offer has expired while you were living. It sounds crazy, but it's true. If you are going to sell your house by yourself, you need a smart phone, and you need it set to annoy you every single time a message from any one of your four to seven email and messaging platforms comes in. Now, more than ever, time is of the essence.

If you have a firm bottom-line, make sure that you have justified that bottom line with strong research. Weigh the cost of marketing the home. Assess if it is worth it for you to sell. If you will lose money to sell your house, a better option might just be to rent it out until the market improves.

If you are shy about haggling with someone who has much more knowledge than you do, consider hiring a professional – a real estate attorney, at least – to assist with your negotiations. Lawyers are more expensive than real estate agents, but they get the job done, too. They are also fiduciaries, and will battle it out with your buyer's agent to get you the best price for your place. This way, you free yourself of the heartache of constantly being two steps behind your adversary.

TIDBIT: Your buyer is your adversary. They are trying to get you to come down to your lowest possible price, and then a little lower. And more often than not, they have a professional agent representing them. Because of your disadvantage, your job is to keep your shirt. But your job is also to get your house sold. That's where the emotional content of the sale comes in. You must remain calm at the center of the storm.

Once you have an offer that is acceptable to you, it is time to go "Pending". Pending means that the sale of your home is in process. You have signed the offer, and returned it to the buyer's agent. This is also the beginning of the escrow period. Your buyer will request an escrow period of a certain number of days. Usually, but by no means always, this escrow period is between thirty and forty-five days. You can always counter with a request for a shorter escrow period. The reason to do this is to shorten the amount of time that your buyer would be able to back out of the sale for any reason, including structural issues with the house, issues that are beyond your control and are not visible to you or the buyer at the time of sale, and issues that you are not interested in dealing with anymore, but that could be a make-or-break for your buyer.

The acceptance and remittance of the accepted offer to the buyer's agent is also the beginning of the inspection period. The inspection period is also defined by the buyer and accepted or rejected by the seller. Generally, the buyer will request an inspection period of ten days. This give them time to hire the necessary inspectors to complete all surveys that will satisfy their requirements of due diligence. This also satisfies the requirements of the buyer's lending institution. These inspections include, but are not limited to:

Home Inspection

Sewerscope

Radon

Soil Inspections

Underground Fuel Tank Inspections

Environmental Surveys

It is very important at this time that you hire a title and escrow company to complete your transaction in a legal fashion that will satisfy the buyer's lender and the local municipal government. This is usually done for a flat percentage rate of the total transaction, and the fee changes with market conditions. At the time of the publishing of this book, the fee is capped at 3%. The title company will do a complete report on the history of the title pertaining to your house, and all rights and obligations that are attached to the property.

From the beginning of escrow, the title company is compiling documents, tax records, plat maps, rental and lease agreements, permit histories, and more, to put together a complete and accurate packet of the necessary materials that will allow you to transfer the title of your property into your buyer's name. Without a title company, it is very difficult to complete a real estate sale. Many necessary documents, documents which you, and even I, have never heard of, would be omitted from the sale, and the result could be catastrophic for you, and also the buyer, when they try to resell the property ten or twenty years down the line.

The buyer has until midnight at the end of the inspection period, or the time specified in the contract, to back out of the deal. They can back out for any reason, and do not need to tell you why they don't want the house. It can be a bad feeling they got from the sewerscope that they saw on youtube that showed a tree branch growing through the sewer line of someone else's house. It could be that they just got cold feet and decided to rent for another five years because they like the pattern of the linoleum in their apartment better than the hard wood floors you are offering. Doesn't matter. They can back out for any reason, until the end of the inspection period. Once the inspection period ends, they are in contract with you, and you are in contract with them. You can't say, "Oh, my granddaughter told me she couldn't live if I sold the house where she learned how to ride a bike". It's done. If you back out, the buyer can sue you for "Specific Performance". That means that you are obligated to perform the agreement that you signed. And likewise, the buyer cannot back out of the contract, without losing their earnest money.

Ahhh... The earnest money. Yes. This is where it becomes critically important to understand that you must not agree to sell your house without a substantial earnest money offer from your buyer. Your buyer will LOSE their earnest money if they bail on you once in contract. You will at least recoup your marketing investment before having to start all over again. The title company will disburse the earnest money to you upon severance of the contract between you and your would-have-been buyer.

Once the inspection period is complete, assuming nothing goes awry, and it's almost certain that something will, then you are in purgatory.............. You just sit. And wait. And wait. And wait--

And then something weird shows up. Your title person calls you and says you're missing a document. Helmut Van Haberstadt had a lease-hold granting him the right to walk across your land in 1922, because his sheep would not adjust their walking path for the owner's property line. If this isn't dissolved, Helmut's ancestors will still have the rights to part of the property that you thought you owned outright!

You have to rush over to the office where that document is located and, guess what? They don't have it. It was on microfiche and has been sent to the hall of records at the state capital. You have to call the state capital and talk to seven receptionists, all of whom have no idea what you're talking about, and eventually you find the hermitic bureaucrat in the basement where all the microfiche is stored, and you get him to go on an epic safari through fifty year-old documents three stories high, to find your necessary item. He does it, though, because he gets that rush that only twenty years in academia can give you, when he finds that elusive file. It takes him three days and nights. He camps out in the basement with power bars and Star Wars branded energy drinks, and he finds your document. He gleefully scans and emails the item to your title person, and you're back on track. Phew. Just in the nick. Until the next bump...

CHAPTER 6. Closing the Deal

TIDBIT: Of all the for-sale-by-owner properties on the market, less than ten percent close. Surprised? Over ninety percent of all FSBO properties end up listed with a broker, often after much hardship and cost to the seller. This is not to say it's impossible. It's just not for the weak at heart. You must be educated, entrepreneurial, a little bit naive, and relentless to make it happen.

First of all, make sure you know your closing paperwork for a home sale in your particular state. Know it backward and forward. Practice filling out the paperwork numerous times prior to closing, so that you understand the terminology, time frames, obligations and rights that are enclosed in the documents which release your interest in the property and declare a new person rightful owner to it. Hopefully, your buyer will have already provided you with their written preapproval, nothing in their financial situation has changed in the month and a half you've been in this deal with them, and you will sail through the closing process. But as I said before, you have to be ready for bumps and knocks the whole way through.

If you have opted out of using a title and escrow company, which I DO NOT recommend, then you should add some flexibility to your closing date. Schedule your own move, and the transfer of possession, so that it's easy for both you and the buyer to accomplish, even if the mortgage approval process gets pushed back.

Be prepared for the results of any home inspections and appraisals, in an unemotional way, and come to the closing table with everything mandated by state and federal law. Use state and federally approved forms, and notarize everything. Notarize, notarize, notarize. Then, immediately go and record the contract. Without recordation, there is no contract between you and the buyer that can be upheld in a court of law should issues arise later.

Hopefully, the buyer has purchased title insurance. This allows you to move forward feeling secure that any previous nonsense with the title will be taken care of without you having liability for errors and omissions regarding the title and its history. Most lenders will require title insurance in order to disburse funds to the borrower.

Once title is closed, you take your money, minus the thousands of dollars in costs, to the bank! You are done! Then you go directly to the travel agency (priceline or travelocity nowadays), and you buy yourself that much-deserved ticket to paradise. Take your Chocolate Lab, or your spouse, with you. She put up with all this nonsense. The people trapsing through your house for months, the strange uniformed men poking and prodding the internal workings of your place, the endless phone calls at all hours from stressed-out people needing information from you. You did it! You got a huge thing done. You sold your house. Congrats.

Was it worth it? Would you do it again, given the choice? If you are one of the ten percent of people who get through the process of selling your home or real property without the help of an agent, I give you mad props. You probably are the kind of person who is just crazy enough to try it a second time. Kudos. I had to go to school, pay thousands in licensing and association fees, take three classes per week, ask countless older brokers for advice, fly blind sometimes, fall on my face a lot, to succeed at buying and selling real estate. My hat is off to you for this achievement. It is truly nothing to shake a stick at.

EPILOGUE: The Psychology

In this book, I have talked a little about the psychology of selling your own home. And it's easy, in the lead-up to making the decision to sell, to ignore some very close-to-home aspects of the process. You will have all kinds of people coming into your life who are complete strangers, being nosy about your business. And that's hard to take sometimes. They will be lawyers, agents, title people, appraisers, inspectors, city bureaucrats, and more, who have no investment in your life or your property. They will not have the slightest clue about what you are going through.

If you have any of the more acute issues that people have, like a tendency to accumulate objects, otherwise known as hoarding, then moving and selling your house can truly be a traumatic experience. This is a situation that I would definitely recommend going through with a therapist at your side, and a real estate agent. Real estate agents are un-licensed therapists. We are accustomed to listening, to helping our clients solve problems, and to facilitating sometimes nearly impossible transactions. There are sales that, for all practical purposes, should never go through. And yet they do. If you have an acute issue, give yourself a break. It's not easy for us to get through it. But it's our chosen profession. It's what we do. Sometimes it's just worth it to pay the bill and move on so that you know it's getting done.

For the rest of you, there will still be things that come up through the course of your house sale that will trigger your emotional reaction. If your couch has occupied the same corner of your living room for twenty years, you married and divorced your husband at the same kitchen table, your kids swam in that pool for their whole childhood, you had that party where your best friend got too drunk and fell in the pool while trying to flirt with your wife's boss and changed the entire course of your life FOREVER!, then selling your house will present its spiritual challenges.

My advice to you all is this: take your time. Get as much knowledge as you can. Use experts to find information. Ask a thousand questions. Be diligent. And most of all: Admit that it's just business.

The market is like the universe. It doesn't have opinions about you, or about what your intentions are. It doesn't think you deserve $350k instead of $299k. It doesn't put expectations like this on you. YOU put expectations on yourself. And the only judge of your success in the end is you. The market is what the market is. It is the judgment, for better or for worse, of the entirety of the people who participate in it. Therefore, it has a larger-scale wisdom than you do regarding the value of your home. While I, as a real estate agent, am not omniscient, the market truly is. Find your place in the market. Find your price. If you are feeling like you NEED to get this, or you HAVE to have that, you are probably too involved. It's time to step back and let it go. Your house will sell.

Just about any house can sell. It doesn't even have to be standing straight upright, necessarily, to fetch a buyer. That's true. But it does have to sell at market value. It's a law. And that's where your desires, your feelings, and your stress, have to subside, and let business be business. Otherwise, you are wasting your own time and energy on something that will never happen.

On the other hand, as an independent agent selling your house yourself, you also have to keep your shirt. And there-in, lies the internal battle that will define you as an entrepreneur, capable of doing your own personal business, or as one of the 90%+ of people who realize that they need help to sell their real estate.

I hope that this book inspires you to be one of the 10% that pull it off. The more decentralized all industries get, the more power the individual has. And I would love for all men and women to be in control of their own destinies. May this book be a stepping stone for you in that quest, as my endeavors in real estate have and continue to be for me.

Peace!

Zachary Rouse
Januray, 2014

P.S. On the next page is some stats on FSBO's and Realtor sales of real estate. Don't be discouraged by the stats. Although they are true and accurate, they refer to the laziest and least motivated home sellers out there. If you are entrepreneurial, as I assume you are because you purchased this book, then these stats will be illuminating to you, and will alert you to things that you need to pay closer attention to when working on your own deal. I included the infographic for your information, not to make you feel like it's an impossible task. It is possible. It's hard. But it is possible. Many people have done it. So can you.

REALTORS VS. FOR SALE BY OWNERS

Is selling your own home without a realtor really cheaper?

FSBO takes 19 more days to sell

Not only do FSBOs empirically take longer to sell, 20% of them end up relisting on MLS which converts to an average of 88 days longer on the market than realtor properties.

For sale by owner = FSBO

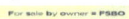

Realtor properties sell for $41,000 more

In 2012 FSBOs accounted for as little as 9% of the property listing and had a significantly lower selling price on average. FSBO properties sold for $174,900 where the realtor properties sold for $215,000.

Total number of property sales by FSBOs has tumbled from 20% to 9% in the last decade

Despite FSBO kits readily available and the power of the internet, the popularity of selling via FSBO in 2012 still declined to just 9%.

70% of FSBOs said they have significant difficulty selling

Based on NAR's 2012 data on FSBO sellers that did not know buyer

Credits and references

www.ingramcontent.com/pod-product-compliance
Lightning Source LLC
Chambersburg PA
CBHW041150180526
45159CB00002BB/762